The ABCs of Women in Music

Written by
Anneli Loepp Thiessen

Illustrated by
Haeon Grace Kang

G-10547
ISBN: 978-1-62277-628-3
Copyright © 2022 GIA Publications, Inc.
7404 S. Mason Ave., Chicago, IL 60638 • www.giamusic.com
This book was printed in March 2022 by RR Donnelley in Dongguan, China.

Dedication

This book is for the women who aren't found on these pages: whose songs were rarely heard, manuscripts forgotten, concerts unattended. We will do better. We all belong in music.

H is for Alexina Louie

Alexina captures the hearts of audiences by telling all kinds of stories with her music. One time she even wrote an opera about burnt toast!

Alexina Louie – Composer (b. 1949)

B is for Beyoncé

Beyoncé knows how to make the world listen. And when they're listening, she sings about how Black Lives Matter and that single ladies are powerful.

Beyoncé Knowles – Pop Singer (b. 1981)

C is for Clara Schumann

Clara decided to be a composer even though all of the other composers around her were men. She knew that music can make our hearts sing and our minds whirl.

Clara Schumann – Composer (1819–1896)

D is for Dolly Parton

When Dolly was a little girl her family was very poor. She shows us that although it will be hard, women can overcome even the toughest obstacles.

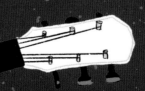

Dolly Parton – Country Singer (b. 1946)

E is for Ella Fitzgerald

Da-ba-do-wee! Ella
was so good at scatting,
or using her voice to
imitate instruments, that
people called her the
Queen of Jazz.

Ella Fitzgerald – Jazz Singer (1917–1996)

F is for Florence Price

Florence wrote over 300 pieces of music with the help of devoted friends who supported her career. She knew the special power of women helping each other out.

Florence Price – Composer (1887–1953)

G is for Gaelynn Lea

Gaelynn is known for her vibrant voice and magical fiddle tunes. She especially loves improvising, or making up music on the spot.

Gaelynn Lea – Violinist, Singer (b. 1984)

H is for Hildegard von Bingen

Hildegard was a visionary. She had fierce dreams about the earth. These visions inspired her to write bold lyrics and enchanting melodies.

Hildegard von Bingen – Composer, Writer (1098–1179)

I is for Isabella Colbran

For a long time, men sang women's parts in operas because women weren't allowed to. Isabella's captivating performances helped set the stage for women to sing.

Isabella Colbran – Opera Singer (1785–1845)

J is for Jada Watson

Jada uses graphs and charts to research the voices we hear on the radio. She helps us understand that we need to listen to more women and people of color.

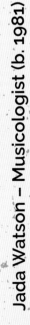Jada Watson – Musicologist (b. 1981)

K is for Kassia

Kassia was a nun who lived over 1,000 years ago. She wrote majestic hymns and songs that we still sing today, showing us that women have always composed.

Kassia – Composer (810–865)

L is for Lizzo

Wherever she performs, Lizzo preaches acceptance. She believes we all deserve to feel good in our bodies and proud of who we love.

Lizzo – Pop Singer, Rapper, and Flautist (b. 1988)

M is for Mary Youngblood

Before Mary came along, only men performed on the Native American flute. Mary transformed the art by becoming the first woman to make recordings on her instrument.

Mary Youngblood – Native American Flautist (b. 1958)

N is for Nannerl Mozart

Many people know about Nannerl's brother but forget that she was also a remarkable composer, spinning brilliant melodies and charming harmonies.

Nannerl Mozart – Composer (1751–1829)

O is for Odetta

Odetta used her mighty voice to reduce division and help Black Americans get equal rights. She is remembered as "the voice of the civil rights movement" because of the way she sang for justice.

Odetta – Activist, Singer (1930–2008)

P is for P!nk

Whether she's singing to a sold out stadium or hanging out at home, P!nk's kids are by her side. Women can be rockstars and moms too!

P!nk – Pop Singer (b. 1979)

Q is for Quilla

As an electronic music producer and DJ, Quilla blends unique sounds and rhythms from around the world in upbeat songs. Her music will make you want to get up and dance!

Quilla – DJ, Producer, and Singer (b. 1982)

R is for Renée Fleming

Some people told Renée she wasn't a good singer, but she didn't listen to them and now she is one of the most famous opera singers in the world.

Renée Fleming – Opera Singer (b. 1959)

S is for Selena

Even though Selena only lived to be 23 years old, she is remembered as one of the most influential Latin singers of all time. She is so beloved that there are even movies about her!

Selena – Pop Singer (1971–1995)

T is for Tanya Tagaq

Tanya sings about things that are hard to talk about. She uses music to fight for women, the planet, and Indigenous rights.

Tanya Tagaq – Inuk Improvisational Singer, Avant-Garde Composer (b. 1975)

U is for Ulali

The women of Ulali know that our voices are strongest together: each voice with its own part, but joined with others to build an irresistible chorus.

Ulali – First Nations A Cappella Ensemble (founded in 1987)

V is for Valerie Capers

Valerie plays piano like nobody's business, inviting everyone to experience the joy of playing jazz. She helps students explore new kinds of music, from blues to bossa nova.

Valerie Capers – Jazz Pianist, Educator (b. 1935)

W is for Wendy Melvoin

Wendy writes dazzling soundtracks for movies and television shows. Her music will keep you on the edge of your seat!

Wendy Melvoin – Composer, Songwriter (b. 1964)

X is for Xian Zhang

All eyes on Xian! As a conductor, everyone in the orchestra follows her lead. She uses her arms to give cues on how to play music: smooth as butter, fast as a racecar, or quiet as a mouse!

Xian Zhang – Conductor (b. 1973)

Y is for Yuja Wang

When Yuja performs she glistens with brilliance and determination. She knows that on and off the stage, women choose and celebrate their own sense of style.

Yuja Wang – Concert Pianist (b. 1987)

Z is for Zenobia Powell Perry

Zenobia was a composer, a teacher, a pianist, and an activist. She wrote many songs, even though only one was published. When women forge their own paths, their voices will be heard.

PASTELS
by: Zenobia Powell Perry

I believe women belong in music!

My name is: _____

My favorite song is: _____

My role model for women in music is: _____

Three words to describe women in music are: _____

I can name women in music.....

One DJ: _____

One conductor: _____

One musicologist: _____

One ensemble: _____

Two pianists: _____

Two pop singers: _____

Two opera singers: _____

Three composers: _____

I know about women in music....

Who plays the Native American flute? _____

Who was known as the Queen of Jazz? _____

Who used her music for change in the civil rights movement? _____

Who writes soundtracks for movies? _____

Who teaches jazz music? _____

Who wrote over 300 pieces of music? _____

Whose music was inspired by her dreams and visions? _____

Who wrote an opera about burnt toast? _____

Who was born the longest time ago? _____

Who was born the most recently? _____

Flip through the book to find the answers. See how much you know about women in music!

Anneli Loepp Thiessen is a PhD student in music living in Ottawa, Ontario, where her research uses an intersectional approach to highlight the important contributions of women in music, noting a diversity of age, race, ability, and orientation. She has been a music teacher for more than 10 years. This is her first children's book.

Haeon Grace Kang is a visual artist from Winnipeg, Manitoba, where she studies theology, marriage and family counseling, and fine arts. She seeks to highlight the diversity of women's bodies, experiences, and backgrounds in her work.

Additional Resources

To find more resources that coordinate with *The ABCs of Women in Music*, visit:

www.giamusic.com/womeninmusic